The Rebel's Cry

M. Therizō

BookLeaf
Publishing

India | USA | UK

Presentation by *BookLeaf Publishing*

Web: www.bookleafpub.com

E-mail: info@bookleafpub.com

ISBN: 9789360943721

First edition 2024

Graffiti Dreams

What is a dream?
Is it a goal or a fantasy?
Is it made on a star
Or in the streets ?
Do we forget it as kids?
Do we live it as adults?
In the sands of time:
Has it been or will it never be?

I suppose that depends on you.
Chalk on the concrete,
But what form did it take?
The hazy memory
 of a dream as we wake.
If you could write your eulogy,
What would it say?
What would you do if
You knew you only had today?

Would you reach for the top?
Would you still fear the drop?
With a life you will lose,
Which path with you choose?
Money and Possessions,
now worthless obsessions.
A final task to go
hatch the dream in your soul.

Growing Pains

It's natural to be afraid of that rip;
Muscles can't grow unless they tear.
Memories, torn down as buildings deconstruct
The plots are filled, but not replaced.
Silence, dead center of the amphitheater
A mime, mockery of life
Trust in a process, despite its strife,
Hibernate with faith in spring.

A crack in the chrysalis
or maybe a catalyst.
The dawn that leads to day
A break in the damn,
trickling, before it explodes.
Hatching from an Egg,
Thrown from the Nest.
Which turn will the River take next?

Photos, burnt to a stench.
Mirrors, scattered to shards.
Voices, blurred to static.
Faces, beyond recognition.
Time marches on.
Forced or willing,
you tag along
Eventually, you move on.

The Flavor of Shimmers

Shimmers at the bottom of a well.
Like a moth drawn to a flame,
head over heels, you dove right in.
Nothing is lighter than the
naivety held by children
but, that didn't break your fall.
No, you crashed head first.
Gasping for air, but tasting Freedom.

The Caged Bird Flew

The caged bird flew
even though they clipped his wings,
He made it through.

Feathers flounced about.
No mouth, but boy,
did he shout!

Never did he glance around.
Soaring high, his only goal:
To never touch the ground.

Garden

In every blooming garden
death can be found
within the leaves
or in the ground.
Often it's needed
to nourish the new
although in can hinder
without a clear view.

In comes a storm
blusters will de-root
chucking flowers around
rain will dilute
and flowers will drown
but maybe it's needed
when the sun arrives
on a garden well-weeded.

Hound Justice

Born and raised in Rot
Knowing only what it's taught
A sickly Dog
Lost in Fog
Stumbled into the street
Crumbled by unknown feet

At the mercy of a Stranger
One would expect danger
The mutt passed out, broken
A new home it awoke in,
For the first time tasting fresh meat
Now knowing the flavour of deceit

Past came knocking at the door
A Liar strolled across the floor
Enraged, the Dog attacked
The Owner ran, mask cracked.
With this paradigm overthrown,
the Hound guards it's new home.

The Final Straw

Water behind a damn,
Light in a star,
Funny how a little
can go so far.

Bursting through wood,
Exploding in space,
With such raw power
there's no time for grace.

Once a whisper,
now a scream.
Once an accident,
now a theme.

So touch the flame,
Poke the bear,
Fight a lion
if you dare.

Planet ≠ Profit

Who told you that you could sell the world?
Who said it was yours to sell?
Billions have lived and died on these lands,
Tell me, what is so special about your hands?

How did you come into possession of a planet?
What stars aligned for that to happen?
Plants wither, mountains weather, waves wash
them away;
Maybe the things we gain aren't meant to stay.

What made you think this was alright?
Tell us, how do you sleep at night?
You steal and sell the dreams of the people,
To fund the illusion that we are all equal.

You play your cards, but what is your game?
Cut us down, but don't we bleed the same?
Behind closed doors, this is how you behave?
When your time comes, I hope you march in
shame to your grave.

Rat Rebellion

Like rats, we scurry and hurry
As rats, we're made for the night.
We scamper through holes
We take from the unattended.

Our colony grows strong
With outcasts who join along.
Tomorrow is a new day
So long to the old way.

Mouse Paradise

We're mice in a colony
where numbers don't shrink,
Our unity is conditional,
dependant on capacity.

All food is limitless
All sickness eliminated
Darwin, denied, but
Even heaven can be hell.

Unable to claw our escape,
We step over bodies.
Bodies of friends and lovers;
Bodies we ended for space.

As We Die

We live as we die
dancing in dazzling flame
refusing to rot away.

Scream into the night
watch the city burn alive
sing along to their demise.

Paint it on the walls.
Nail it to the church.
We live as we die.

The Birth of an Island

Volcanic slam poetry
Angry mountain song
Spewing to the heavens
Sealing to the depths.

Rhythmic serenity
Tides of senses
Mingling with lava
Building new land.

Burnt Perspective

You left me to die
in the ashes
of a world you broke.

Heaving and gagging,
I spat the smoke out;
I survived.

I learned you're a city
not a home.

I learned you're a city
not the world.

From Dusk to Dust

Shattered stars
refracted through space,
An atmosphere
dyed by dream dust.
Atop a hill of dying grass
yearning for clouds above,
Like a mother on a lamp
on the outside looking in.

Oh to be wind,
Fresh, flowing.
Shame to be stone,
aged, stagnant,
Caked in dirt;
Dirt that clings.
The kind that never
truly washes out.

There's a solace in waves
that can was yesterday away,
but no one can breathe underwater.
Even if they scream.
Wait a little, wait a while,
wait forever and you'll die.
Tides retreat, as does the moon,
All must emerge eventually.

The sun, a cruel keeper
demands another day.
Blinding light
ushers in colour,
Scorching heat
summons life,
Survive until night
to rest among stars.

Knight's Lullaby

Lay down your sword love;
Carry it tomorrow, not tonight.
Stay with us, halt your flight.
The battle has just begun,
the war is yet to end.
The worst has yet to come;
rest until then.

For years you've fought,
lay your armor down.
Stay, let us repair
the cracks in your skin;
Let us make you whole again.
We'll lend you our strength,
and watch your soar with pride.

In life you won't keep much;
losing swords and soldiers alike.
But not us, never us.
Bound tightly by red string
in braids that cannot untie.
By your side we grew
and by it, we'll die.

Contemplation

I've scratched and scratched
until my claws ripped out.

I've bitten and screamed
until my jaw broke.

Left in the wasted rubble
of my tragic, broken body.

Was the pain inflicted
worth all I've reflected?

Siren Song

Dream of all you could be
Dream of me
Ease into sleep
Ease into my grasp

Dream of success
Dream of Utopia
Fall away from worry
Fall deep into slumber

Dream a little longer
Dream your life away
Listen to my lullaby
Listen to my command

Dream of glory
Dream of me
Abandon all caution
Abandon all choice

Dream of me
And only me
My clueless pet
My precious cattle
Dream.
  Dream.
    Dream.

Before You Wake

Thrashing, screaming.
Unable to wake.
Battling monsters,
A life at stake.

No where to go
but deeper in.
The strange feeling
of re-arranging skin.

Lean into the darkness.
Let the laughter drag you down.
Bathe in the ether,
Give in, go drown.

Head first in the pool
There's light at the bottom.
Breathe in the water
end up in Sodom.

Dance through the rubble.
Awake from rebirth,
that you find as you rest
in the soil of the earth.

Dis(connect)

Some day the children will sever
the cords you placed in their ears.
Then, they'll hear
your honest thoughts.

Eventually, those kids will unravel
the bandages over their eyes.
Thus they'll see
your real intentions.

Soon that generation will speak
with voices you couldn't silence.
Armed with the knowledge
of true noise and sight.

The Rebel's Cry

We are Rebels, hear us cry
our voices carry, long after we die
We are rebels, feel our force
we were birthed by your lack of remorse
We are rebels, here we stand
between your greed and our homeland
We are rebels, it's best if you skip town
fists in the air, we will burn corruption down
We are rebels, but that's not all that we are
we are the stab from society that left a scar
We are rebels, I dare you to lock us away
so you can watch our martyrs grow by the day
We are rebels, we will always be here
we are the the warm chaos to your cold "order"
and we will not disappear.

Ending Scene

Reduced to dust
Voyaging on wind
Scattered through space,
Ground, lost to sight.

The map knows not my location,
Nor does the compass my direction
The stars know not my language,
Still they try to guide me.

On tomorrow, I draw a blank
There is only here and now
The past too, slipped away,
In this hour glass, I lie alone.